MW01629435

To Chynna, Riccardo, Matteo, and children all around the world,
I encourage you to find your passion and follow your dreams.

And to Angela, thank you for your endless
encouragement and support.

KEEP DREAMIN'
Steph

For Katie, with love

www.katiesreaders.org

Reach for the Stars

Written by Steph Blore

Illustrations by Cheryl Ferrari

Katie's Readers

The things you can do are varied by far,

You can ride a bike, you can drive a car.

Sail a boat or fly a plane.

You only need to use your brain.

You could build a house or write a book,

Sing on a stage or become a cook.

Design some clothes, get into fashion –

Whatever you do, find your passion.

Travel the world and see all the sights,

Be an activist for human rights.

Act in a play, make a movie –

All these things are really groovy.

Work in construction or become a plumber.

If music's your thing, you could be a drummer!

Most important of all is to find what you love,

Then whatever you choose will fit like a glove.

A lawyer, a dentist or even a dancer,

A fireman, a baker – you will find the answer.

A journalist working for a national newspaper.

Or a banker who works in a towering skyscraper.

"A doctor," you say. Then I say "Why not?"

A captain who sails the high seas on a yacht.

A farmer who tends to his cows and his sheep.

A tour guide who drives you around in a jeep.

You may become a husband or wife,

Bring little children in to your life.

You may even find yourself on Mars,

So, follow your heart and reach for the stars!

Believe you can and follow your dreams,

It may not be as hard as it seems!

And if it's harder than you thought,

Just remember what you've been taught:

To do what you love and love what you do,

Believe in yourself – your dreams will come true.

With a goal in your mind and love in your heart,

You're already off to a wonderful start!

Writer

When I was a child I loved to read; there was nothing quite like burying my nose inside a book and having the story transport me to another place and time. I love holding a book and turning its pages, anticipating what might happen next. The more books I read, the more I began to dream about writing a book myself one day.

I started my writing journey many years later while working in the travel industry. I spent many hours in airports waiting for flights, observing people while jotting down ideas and stories.When I shared those stories with my family they encouraged me to pursue my dream. I am now so excited to be sharing my first book, which inspires young children to never give up on *their* dreams. As you can see, **dreams do come true.**

KEEP DREAMIN'

Steph

Artist

I've always loved to draw, color, and paint. From the time I was very young I would redraw cartoon characters from comic books, like Betty and Veronica of Archie comics. I didn't have a mentor then. People just thought it was a cute hobby. Not until I was in my fifties did I start painting seriously and professionally. Now I'm an artist and illustrator whose fine art paintings and book images are owned by people all over the world. My only wish is that I had started so much sooner. If you have a gifted child, in music, dance, acting, or art, please encourage them. If you can't further them along, please find someone who can be their mentor. The arts are such an important balance, a way to express beauty and passion. The world needs more.

Cheryl

www.cherylynn-art.com/

Extras!

For more inspiration, I have created some activities that complement

Reach for the Stars

which can be found over on my website.

www.stephblore.com

Be sure to share the pages with me on Instagram

@stephblore   #reachforthestars

or email them to me so I can cheer you on!!

steph@stephblore.com

You can also find lots of activities on the Katie's Readers website

www.katiesreaders.org

for this and other books.

ISBN 978-1-8383055-0-5

Made in the USA
Las Vegas, NV
26 April 2022